Music Theory in Practice

Grade 5

ERIC TAYLOR

The Associated Board of the Royal Schools of Music

Syllabus for Grade 5

As in preceding grades, with the addition of:

(1) Irregular time signatures of $\frac{5}{4}$ $\frac{7}{4}$ $\frac{5}{8}$ $\frac{7}{8}$, and the grouping of notes and rests within these times. Irregular division of simple time values.

(2) Tenor clef (C clef centred on 4th line). The identification of notes in the four clefs in any of the keys set for this grade, and the transposition at the octave of a simple melody from any clef to another. The writing at concert pitch of a melody notated for an instrument in B♭, A or F, and vice versa (the interval of transposition up or down will be given). The writing in open score, using treble and bass clefs, of a passage for SATB written on two staves, and vice versa.

(3) Scales and key signatures of all major and minor keys up to six sharps and flats. All simple and compound intervals from any note.

(4) The identification of $\frac{5}{3}$ and $\frac{6}{3}$ chords on the tonic, supertonic, subdominant and dominant in any of the keys set for this grade. The identification of the $\frac{6}{4}$ chord and of the progression $\frac{6}{4}$ $\frac{5}{3}$ on the dominant note in any of the keys set for this grade. The choice of suitable chords using any recognised method of notation at cadential points of a simple melody in the major keys of C, G, D or F.

(5) The composition of a simple melody of not more than eight bars, using a given opening and writing for a specific instrument (some choice will be given) *or* (at candidate's choice) the composition of a melody to given words. Appropriate performing directions relating to tempo, dynamics and articulation will be required.

(6) More terms and signs. The recognition of ornaments, including the replacement of written-out ornamentation with the appropriate signs, but not vice versa. Questions about a passage of music written for voices or instruments will include questions on the types of voice and names of instruments, the clefs they use, instrument family groups and the basic way by which they produce sound, as well as points of general musical observation designed to test the candidate's ability to apply theoretical knowledge to actual music.

First published in 1990 by
The Associated Board of the Royal Schools of Music (Publishing) Ltd

©1990 The Associated Board of the Royal Schools of Music

Reprinted in 1991 (with revisions), 1992, 1994, 1996, 1997, 1998, 2000, 2001, 2002

ISBN 1 85472 494 0

Typesetting and music processing by Halstan & Co. Ltd, Amersham, Bucks
Printed in Great Britain by Headley Brothers Ltd, Ashford, Kent

Contents

Thanks are due to the following for permission to reprint extracts
from copyright works: Boosey & Hawkes Music Publishers Ltd;
Breitkopf & Härtel; Editions Durand S.A./United Music Publishers Ltd;
David Higham Associates Ltd; Editions Hamelle, Paris/United Music
Publishers Ltd; Editions Henn, Switzerland/United Music Publishers Ltd;
Novello & Co. Ltd; Oxford University Press; Peters Edition Ltd;
Schott & Co. Ltd.

The music on the cover is the opening of an arrangement
for trumpet in D and piano by Philip Cranmer of the aria,
'The trumpet shall sound', from Handel's *Messiah*
(*Handel and Bach Arias*, published by the Associated Board)

In the quoted music examples, tempo marks without brackets occur
in the original as shown. Tempo marks in brackets occur earlier in the
music or are editorial.

A   Irregular time signatures

(see *The AB Guide to Music Theory*, 1/2 and 5/3)

An 'irregular' bar is one which cannot be divided into equal groups of two or three beats. The most common are those containing five beats (quintuple time) and seven beats (septuple time). Examples of their time signatures are:

$\frac{5}{4}$ (five crotchets in a bar) $\frac{7}{4}$ (seven crotchets in a bar)

$\frac{5}{8}$ (five quavers in a bar) $\frac{7}{8}$ (seven quavers in a bar)

In Grade 5, the only irregular time signatures will be those listed above. Examples requiring the addition of bar-lines or time signatures raise no new problems: they are simply a matter of counting.

Exercise 1   Add bar-lines to the following examples, which all begin on the first beat of the bar.

d'Indy, *Du Rythme*, Op.68 No.10

(a) **Assez vite**   *p*

Reproduced by permission of Editions Henn, Switzerland/United Music Publishers Ltd

Prokofiev, Piano Sonata No.7 (3rd mvt)

(b) **Precipitato**   *mp*

©Boosey & Hawkes Music Publishers Ltd

Stravinsky, *Petrouchka* ('Masqueraders')

(c) ♩♩. = 72   *f ben cant.*

©Boosey & Hawkes Music Publishers Ltd

Holst, *The Planets* ('Mars')

(d) **Allegro**   *fff*

Copyright © J. Curwen & Sons Ltd

Exercise 2   Add time signatures to the following examples, which all begin on the first beat of the bar.

[Giocoso]   Glière, *Sketch*, Op.47 No.3

(a)   *f*

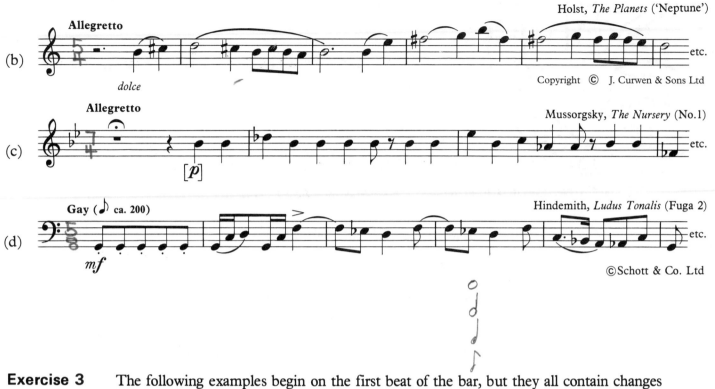

Holst, *The Planets* ('Neptune')

Allegretto

(b)

dolce

Allegretto

Mussorgsky, *The Nursery* (No.1)

(c)

[*p*]

Gay (♪ ca. 200)

Hindemith, *Ludus Tonalis* (Fuga 2)

(d)

mf

Exercise 3 The following examples begin on the first beat of the bar, but they all contain changes of time signature. Add time signatures where they are needed.

Shostakovich, String Quartet No.2 (2nd mvt)

(a)

Moderato

Stravinsky, Octet for Wind Instruments (2nd mvt)

(b)

Copland, Duo for Flute and Piano (2nd mvt)

(c)

B Tenor clef

(see *The AB Guide to Music Theory*, 4/7)

Both the alto and tenor clefs are C clefs (𝄡): the only difference between them is their position on the stave. In the alto clef (which was introduced in Grade 4) middle C is on the third line: but in the tenor clef middle C is on the fourth line:

Key signatures of up to five sharps or flats are arranged thus:

The tenor clef may be used by cellos, bassoons and tenor trombones; it is no longer used in vocal music.

Exercise 4 Underneath each of these notes write its letter name.

Name A......E......C......F......C......F......B......D......G......D......G......B......E......

Exercise 5 After each clef, write the key signature and tonic chord of the given key.

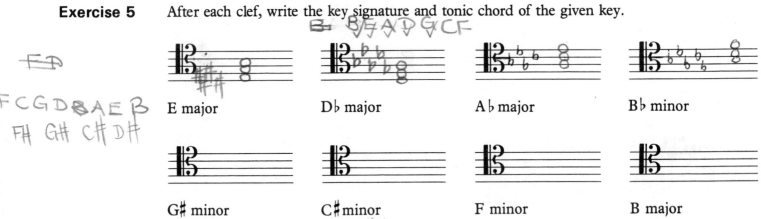

FCGDBAEB
F♯ G♯ C♯ D♯

E major D♭ major A♭ major B♭ minor

G♯ minor C♯ minor F minor B major

Exercise 6 Rewrite each of these passages at the same pitch, using either the treble or bass clef as indicated. Include any given performance directions.[1]

Glinka, *Ruslan and Ludmila* (Overture)

(a)

Presto

mf cantabile

[1]This should always be done in similar exercises.

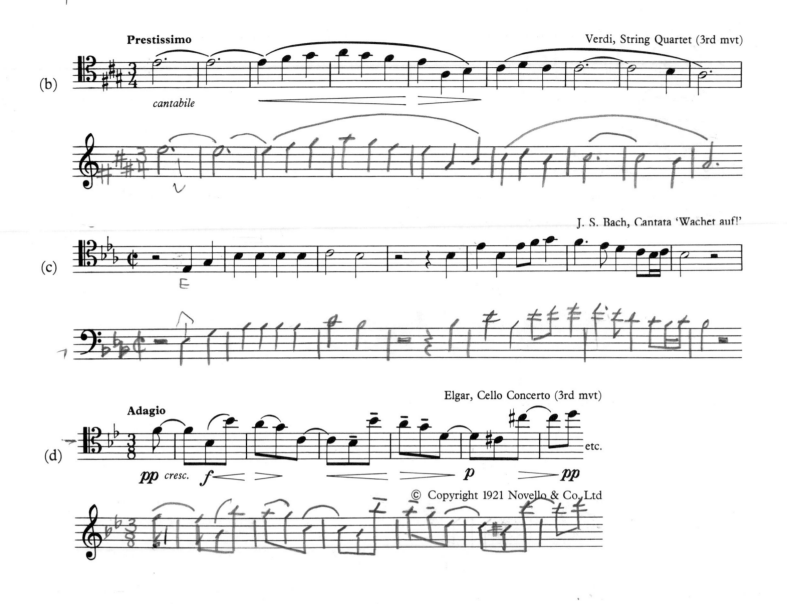

Exercise 7 Rewrite these examples at the same pitch in the tenor clef.

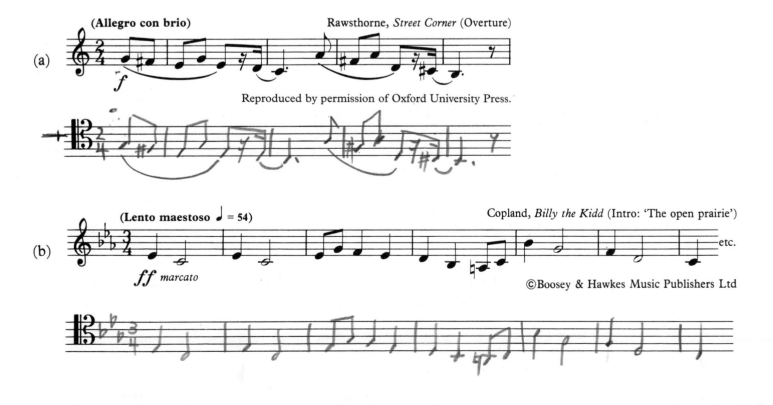

Exercise 7
(continued)

(c) R. Strauss, *Till Eulenspiegel*

©1895 by Josef Aibl Musikverlag. Copyright assigned 1932 to C.F. Peters. Reproduced by permission.

(d) Wagner, *Tannhäuser* (Overture)

(e) Beethoven, String Quartet, Op.131 (2nd mvt)

C Major and minor keys up to six sharps and flats

(see *The AB Guide to Music Theory*, 4/1–3)

Keys with up to five sharps or flats were included in Grade 4. The keys with six sharps are F♯ major and D♯ minor; and the keys with six flats are G♭ major and E♭ minor.

Notice that F♯ major and G♭ major are enharmonic equivalents: their scales *sound* the same although they are *written* differently:

F♯ major

G♭ major

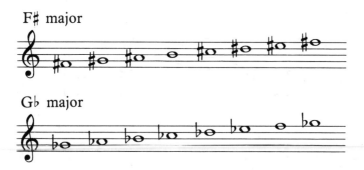

Similarly, D♯ minor and E♭ minor are enharmonic equivalents:

D♯ harmonic minor

(the descending form uses the same notes)

E♭ harmonic minor

(the descending form uses the same notes)

D♯ melodic minor

E♭ melodic minor

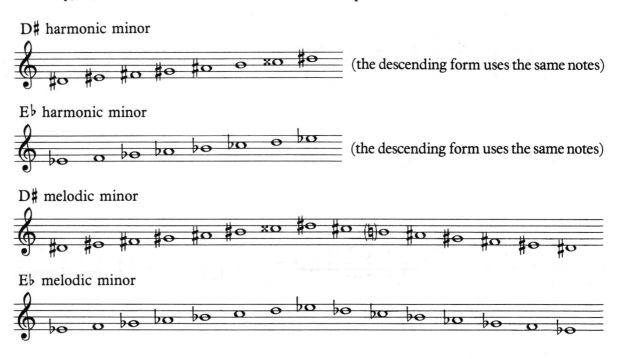

Composers sometimes write pieces (or, more commonly, passages *within* pieces) in more complicated keys: e.g. seven sharps (C♯ major/A♯ minor) or seven flats (C♭ major/A♭ minor). But these extreme keys are generally avoided, because there are simpler enharmonic equivalents. C♯ major, for example, is more easily written as D♭ major (five flats instead of seven sharps). D♯ minor, too, is rare: composers generally prefer to write in E♭ minor.

Key signatures with six sharps or flats are arranged thus:

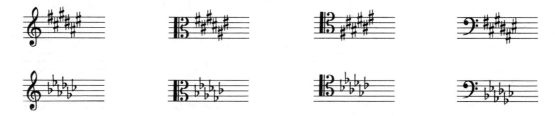

Exercise 8   Add accidentals where needed to make the given scales. (Do not use key signatures.)

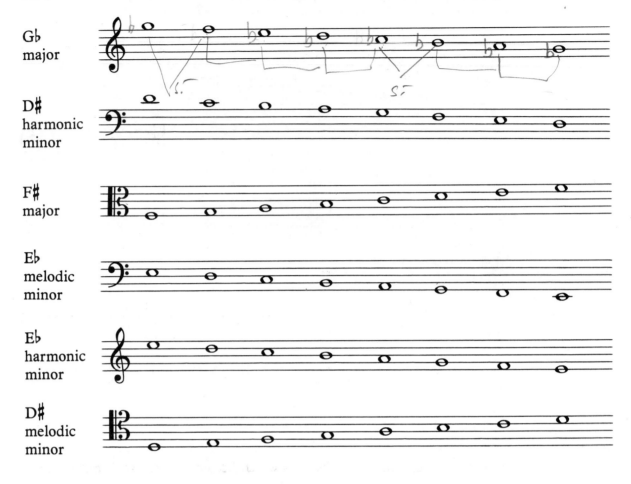

G♭ major

D♯ harmonic minor

F♯ major

E♭ melodic minor

E♭ harmonic minor

D♯ melodic minor

Exercise 9   Add the clefs and accidentals needed to make the given scales. (Do not use key signatures.)

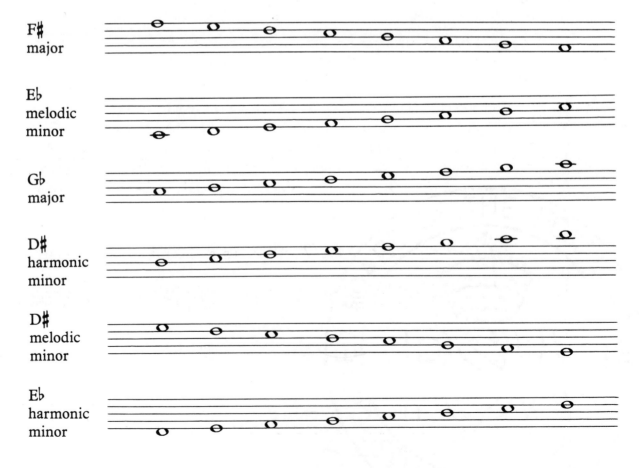

F♯ major

E♭ melodic minor

G♭ major

D♯ harmonic minor

D♯ melodic minor

E♭ harmonic minor

Exercise 10 After each clef write the key signature, followed by the tonic triad, in the given keys.

F♯ major

D♯ minor

G♭ major

E♭ minor

Exercise 11 Name the key of each of the following. Then rewrite them, using the correct key signatures. Remove any accidentals which become unnecessary, but remember also to add any that may be needed. F C G D A E B

(a) *(Poco lento e grazioso)*

Dvořák, *Humoreske*, Op.101 No.7

f *dimin.* *p* etc.

Key .....D♭.mj... ♯ B♭ E♭ A♭ D♭ G♭ C♭ B.E.A.D.G.C.

G♭major

J.S. Bach, 48 Preludes & Fugues, Bk II (Fugue No.8)

(b)

etc. MINOR

Key .....F♯.mj.?... F C G D A E B F♯ G♯ D♯ A♯ E♯ F.C.G.D.A.E = D♯ minor

F C G D A A E etc.

Exercise 11
(continued)

Tchaikovsky, Overture '1812'

Allegro giusto

(c)

p cre — — scen — do etc.

Key F# minor..

Rachmaninov, *Élégie*, Op.3 No.1

Moderato

(d)

mf

Key Eb min.
same as Gb maj.

B E D G C

Puccini, *Madam Butterfly* ('One fine day')

Andante molto calmo

(e)

Key Db maj.

B E A D G

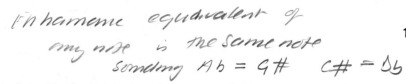

Enharmonic equivalent of any note is the same note sounding Ab = G# C# = Db

Exercise 12   (i) Rewrite the following enharmonically, using key signatures of six sharps, but without changing the sound.

(ii) Rewrite the following enharmonically, using key signatures of six flats, but without changing the sound. (Notice the change of clef in the second example.)

D Transposition

(see *The AB Guide to Music Theory*, 7/2)

You will be asked to transpose a melody. Any of the following intervals may be required:

(1) up or down an octave;
(2) up or down a major 2nd;
(3) up or down a minor 3rd;
(4) up or down a perfect 5th.

These are the intervals most frequently used by transposing instruments in the orchestra[1]. In this Section we will deal with each of them in turn.

(1) *Transposition up or down an octave.* This was introduced in Grade 3, where only the treble and bass clefs were used. In Grade 5, the alto and tenor clefs are also required. Provided you have become familiar with these clefs there should be no difficulty – but make sure that you do actually *transpose* the passage (rather than merely rewrite it at the same pitch in the different clef), and also that you transpose it *one* octave and not two.

Exercise 13 Write this passage an octave lower in each of the given clefs.

[1]See *The AB Guide to Music Theory*, Part II, 19 & 20 (especially 20/2)

Exercise 14 Write this passage an octave higher in each of the given clefs.

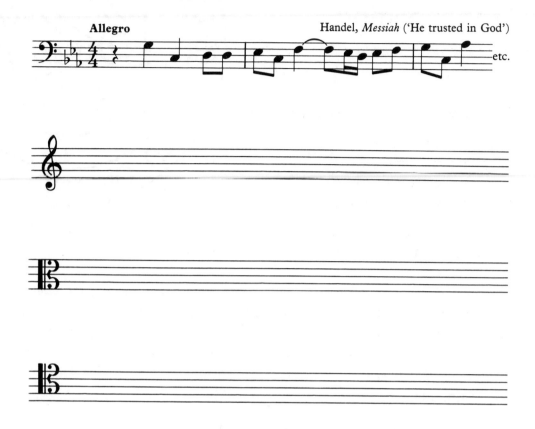

Exercise 15 Write this passage an octave higher in the treble clef, and an octave lower in the bass clef.

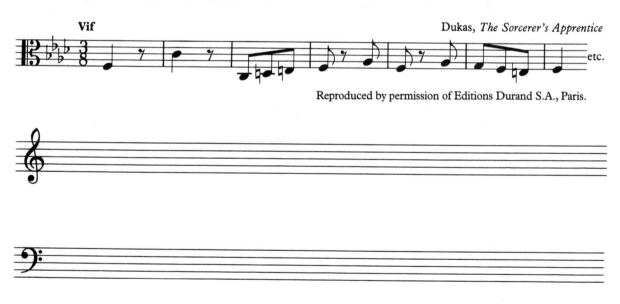

Exercise 16   Write this passage an octave higher in the treble clef, and an octave lower in the bass clef.

J.S. Bach, B minor Mass (Kyrie)

(2) *Transposition up or down a major second.* When instruments 'in B flat'
(e.g. clarinets in B♭, trumpets in B♭) play middle C, the B♭ below it is heard.
In other words, instruments in B♭ produce sounds a major 2nd lower
than the written notes. For example, a melody notated thus –

would actually sound –

And to produce these sounds –

they would have to be written a major 2nd higher for an instrument in B♭ –

The pitch at which the music is actually heard is called 'concert pitch'.

As can be seen in the above examples, not only are the notes transposed but also
the key signatures.

Care is also needed over accidentals occurring during the course of a melody. Note that:

(i) An accidental may have to be changed in the transposed version: e.g. the F natural in the first example opposite becomes E *flat* in the transposed version.

(ii) A chromatically altered note must be replaced by its exact equivalent and not by an enharmonic substitute. (It is true that, for various special reasons, composers do occasionally use enharmonic substitutes, but these are exceptions.) The F natural in the first example opposite (flattened 7th in G major) becomes E flat in the transposed version (flattened 7th in F major) – not D sharp.

Until the early 20th century, horn and trumpet parts were written without a key signature, whatever the key: accidentals were added before individual notes as necessary. Later composers have sometimes used key signatures. In the following exercises, and in examination papers, you should assume that a key signature is to be used unless there is an instruction to the contrary (as in Exercise 23 below).

Except where a transposed part is written without a key signature (as in Exercise 23), *every* accidental in the original requires a corresponding accidental in the transposed version. Do not 'improve' on the given music by omitting to include an accidental where one in the original was not strictly necessary. (It may have been put there as a sensible precaution, e.g. something being played by another instrument might cause confusion.)

The following exercises provide practice in these transpositions. Remember to make the necessary changes to key signatures. As a model, the solution to the opening of the first example in each exercise in this Section is given.

Exercise 17   These passages are notated for instruments in B♭. Write them out at concert pitch, i.e. a major 2nd lower.

Exercise 17
(continued)

Weber, Clarinet Concerto No.1 (1st mvt)

Exercise 18 Transpose these passages up a major 2nd, so that they will sound at concert pitch when played by instruments in B♭.

(3) *Transposition up or down a minor 3rd.* The concert pitch of instruments 'in A' is a minor 3rd lower than written: e.g. when a clarinet in A or a trumpet in A plays middle C, the A below is heard. Thus music written in C major would sound in A major. Similarly, music whose concert pitch is C major would have to be written in E♭ major.

Exercise 19   These passages are notated for instruments in A. Write them out at their concert pitch, i.e. a minor 3rd lower.

(a) Cornet in A — Elgar, *Pomp and Circumstance* March No.1
© 1901 by Boosey & Co. Ltd
Reproduced by permission of Boosey & Hawkes Music Publishers Ltd.

(b) Clarinet in A — Schumann, *Fantasiestücke*, Op.73 No.1

(c) Clarinet in A — Bliss, Clarinet Quintet (1st mvt)
©Novello & Co. Ltd

Exercise 20   Transpose these passages up a minor 3rd, so that they will sound at concert pitch when played by instruments in A.

(a) — Brahms, Symphony No.4 (2nd mvt)

Clarinet in A

Exercise 20
(continued)

**Clarinet
in A**

(4) *Transposition up or down a perfect 5th.* Instruments 'in F' produce the note F ('concert F') when C is played. The most common examples are the horn (i.e. French horn) in F, and the cor anglais. Both sound the F below the C: their notes sound a perfect 5th lower than the written notes, and their parts are written a perfect 5th above the concert notes.

Exercise 21   These passages are notated for instruments in F. Write them out at their concert pitch, i.e. a perfect 5th lower.

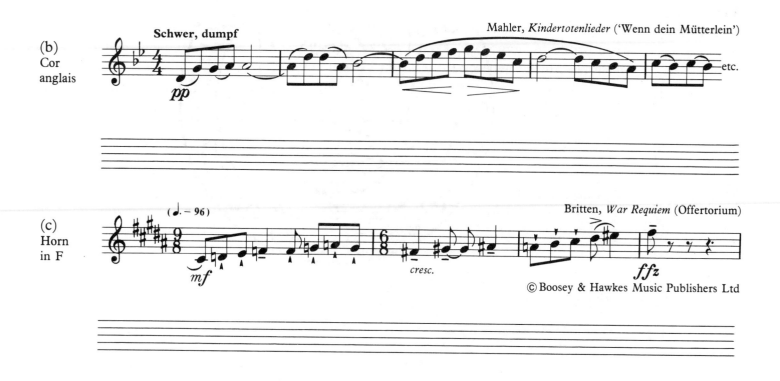

Exercise 22 Transpose the following passages up a perfect 5th, so that they will sound at concert pitch when played by instruments in F. Use treble or bass clefs, as convenient.

Exercise 23   Transpose the following passages up a perfect 5th, so that they will sound at concert pitch when played by horns in F. Do not use key signatures. Add accidentals before all notes which need them: unnecessary accidentals should not be included.

Rachmaninov, Piano Concerto No.1 (3rd mvt)

©Boosey & Hawkes Music Publishers Ltd

Sibelius, Symphony No.2 (2nd mvt)

©Breitkopf & Härtel

Delius, *Walk to the Paradise Garden*

© Copyright 1910 by Hawkes & Son (London) Ltd
Reproduced by permission of Boosey & Hawkes Music Publishers Ltd

E Voices in score

(see *The AB Guide to Music Theory*, Part II, 14/2)

The most usual combination of mixed voices is soprano, alto, tenor and bass (SATB for short). Their music is written either on two staves or on four. In a two-stave layout, the upper voices (soprano and alto) are written on the top stave in the treble clef, with the two lower parts (tenor and bass) on the bottom stave in the bass clef. In a four-stave layout, each part has its own stave. When different vocal parts (e.g. soprano and alto) share a stave, the music is said to be written in 'short score'; and when each of them has a stave of its own, the music is in 'open score'. The staves are usually given separate bar-lines, both in open and in short scores:

You may be required to transcribe into open score a passage written in short score, or vice versa. The above examples illustrate three important points:

(1) In short score the tenor part is written in the bass clef (at its true pitch); but in open score it is written in the treble clef, an *octave higher* than it actually sounds. (You should adopt the modern practice of writing a small 8 under the tenor's treble clef to show that the music sounds an octave lower than written.)

(2) In short score the stems of soprano and tenor notes always go up, wherever they may lie on the stave; similarly, the stems of alto and bass notes always go down.

(3) When two vocal lines share the same stave, an accidental before a note in one part must be written again if the same note occurs in the other part later in the same bar. Thus the second ♯ (to the G) in the two-stave example is necessary although, if this had been piano music, it would not have been.

Exercise 24 Transcribe the following passages into short score. (As a model, the solution to the opening of the first example is given.)

(a)

Purcell, Anthem 'Rejoice in the Lord alway'

J.S. Bach, Chorale 'Wer weiss, wie nahe mir' (Cantata 166)

(b)

Exercise 25   Transcribe the following passages into open score. (As a model, the solution to the opening of the first example is given.)

F More irregular time divisions

(see *The AB Guide to Music Theory*, 5/5a)

The most common irregular time divisions have already been considered: triplets (in Grade 2) and duplets (in Grade 4). The next two exercises provide practice in the use of some more elaborate groups. Notice that, in all of them, the irregular group replaces a 'simple time' unit (i.e. one which would normally divide into 2, 4, 8 etc.). A group of 5, 6 or 7 uses the same time values as a group of 4; and a group of 9 uses the same values as a group of 8.

Exercise 26   Complete the following sentences by adding ♪ or ♩ or 𝅗𝅥 at the end of each.

Exercise 27   Add bar-lines to the following examples, which all begin on the first beat of the bar.

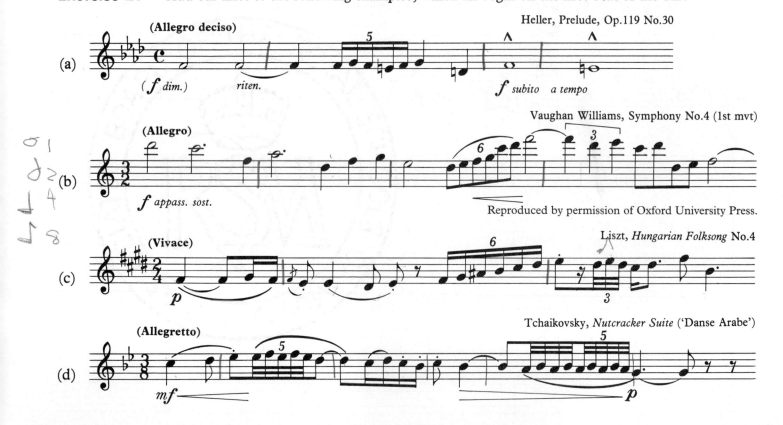

Haydn, Variations (for piano), Hob.XVII/6

(e)

Britten, *Serenade for tenor, horn & strings* ('Dirge')

(f)

Walton, Symphony No.1 (1st mvt)

(g)

Reproduced by permission of Oxford University Press.

Lili Boulanger, *Nocturne*

(h)

G Intervals

(see *The AB Guide to Music Theory*, 7/1 & 3)

The intervals to be described in Grade 5 may be between *any* two notes, including notes which are more than an octave apart.

With regard to intervals of less than an octave, the fact that any two notes may be used raises no new problems. The intervals can still be analysed in the ways described in Grade 4. This, for example, is always a diminished 5th –

whatever the key signature (if there is one) –

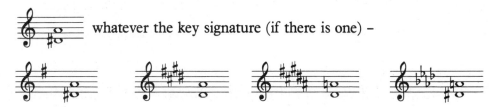

Intervals of more than one octave are 'compound' intervals, described in two ways, e.g.

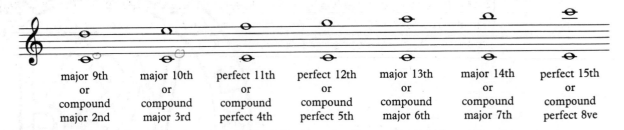

major 9th	major 10th	perfect 11th	perfect 12th	major 13th	major 14th	perfect 15th
or	or	or	or	or	or	or
compound	compound	compound	compound	compound	compound	compound
major 2nd	major 3rd	perfect 4th	perfect 5th	major 6th	major 7th	perfect 8ve

For various reasons, some of these descriptions are used more frequently than
others. Musicians generally refer to a '9th', '10th', '12th' and '15th' rather than to a
'compound 2nd' or a 'compound 3rd' etc. However, in the examination both types of
description are acceptable.

Exercise 28 Above each of these notes write the note needed to produce the given interval.

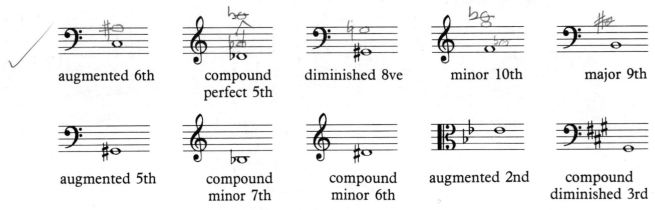

augmented 6th   compound   diminished 8ve   minor 10th   major 9th
                 perfect 5th

augmented 5th   compound   compound   augmented 2nd   compound
                 minor 7th   minor 6th   diminished 3rd

Exercise 29 Describe fully each of these intervals, e.g. augmented 4th, minor 10th (or compound
minor 3rd) etc. Remember always to note the key signature, in case it affects either
of the notes forming the interval.

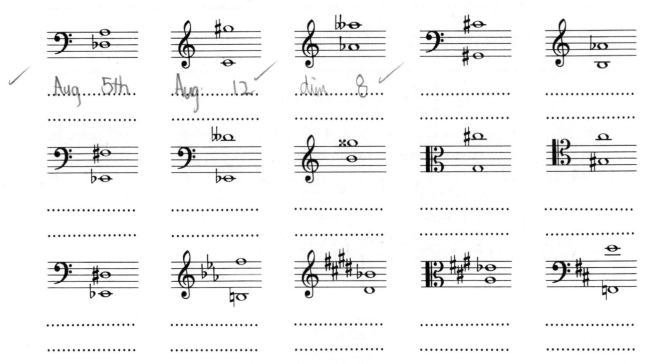

Exercise 30 Describe fully each of the intervals marked ⌐1⌐ ⌐2⌐ etc. in the following passages. (Keep in mind the key signature and any accidentals which may have occurred earlier in the bar. Remember, too, that an interval in a melody is still calculated from the lower note, even if the higher note happens to come first.)

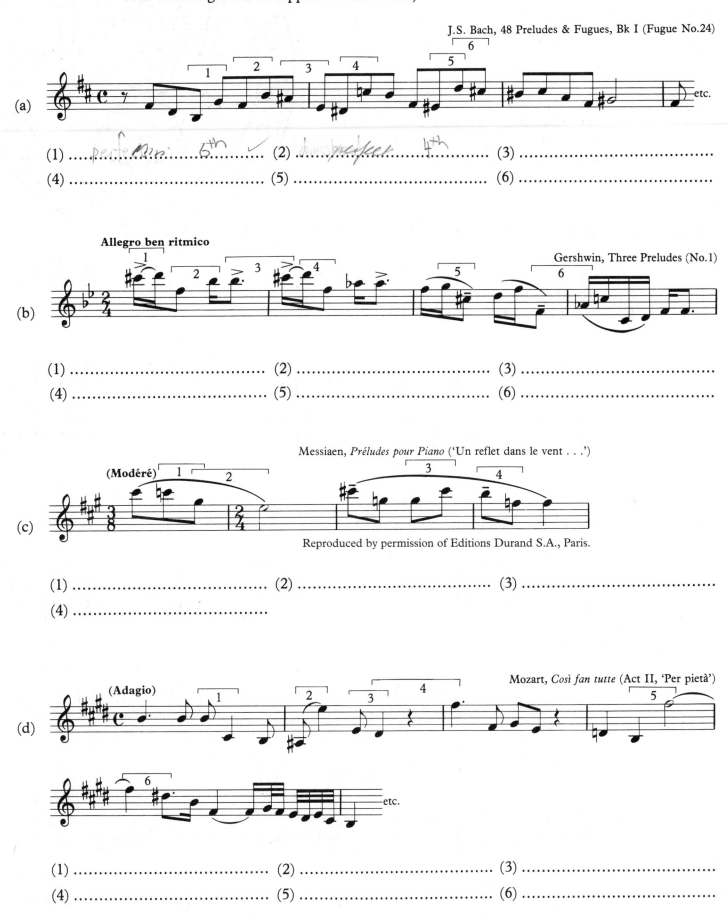

J.S. Bach, 48 Preludes & Fugues, Bk I (Fugue No.24)

(a)

(1) ......perfe min 5th ✓.... (2) ...im perfect 4th.... (3) ....

(4) .... (5) .... (6) ....

Allegro ben ritmico

Gershwin, Three Preludes (No.1)

(b)

(1) .... (2) .... (3) ....

(4) .... (5) .... (6) ....

Messiaen, *Préludes pour Piano* ('Un reflet dans le vent . . .')

(Modéré)

(c)

Reproduced by permission of Editions Durand S.A., Paris.

(1) .... (2) .... (3) ....

(4) ....

Mozart, *Così fan tutte* (Act II, 'Per pietà')

(Adagio)

(d)

(1) .... (2) .... (3) ....

(4) .... (5) .... (6) ....

Exercise 31   Below is a passage for alto and bass soloists, taken from Purcell's *Te Deum* in D. Name the intervals between the two voices at the points indicated by dotted lines.

(1) ....   (2) ....   (3) ....

(4) ....   (5) ....   (6) ....

H Naming chords

(see *The AB Guide to Music Theory*, 8/2)

The chords to be identified in Grade 4 were the tonic (I), subdominant (IV) and dominant (V): all in root position. Grade 5 adds the supertonic (II). You will also be asked which note is in the bass (root, 3rd or 5th) or, to put it another way, which inversion the chord is in. There are various ways of showing this. The most economical is to add 'a', 'b' or 'c' (meaning root position, first inversion and second inversion respectively) to the roman figure denoting the chord. Thus –

Ia = tonic chord in root position;
Ib = tonic chord in first inversion;
Ic = tonic chord in second inversion.

Alternatively, you may write $\frac{5}{3}$ instead of 'a', $\frac{6}{3}$ instead of 'b', and $\frac{6}{4}$ instead of 'c' after the roman figure. The figures here refer to intervals from the bass note: IV$\frac{6}{3}$, for example, = the first inversion of the subdominant chord.

It is very common to indicate a root-position chord by the roman figure alone – e.g. just II (without either 'a' or ' $\frac{5}{3}$ '). If you add nothing to the roman figure, therefore, it will be assumed that you mean a root-position chord.

Here is an example of what is required in Exercise 32 below:

Key: B♭ major   IIb   V   I

Any equivalent of the above chord symbols is acceptable, provided it is clear what is meant and fully describes the function of the chord in the key.

Exercise 32   Name the keys of the following passages. Identify the chords marked with *, and indicate which of the notes is in the bass (or which position the chord is in).

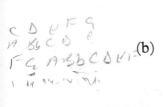

Mendelssohn, Song without Words, Op.102 No.3

(a)

Key ....

Mozart, *The Magic Flute* (Act II, March)

(b)

Key ....

J.S. Bach, Chorale 'Wer nur den lieben Gott lässen' (Cantata 88)

(c)

etc.

Key ....

Exercise 32
(continued)

Key ....

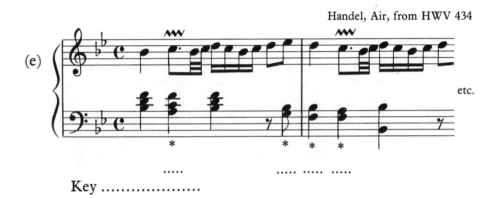

Key ....

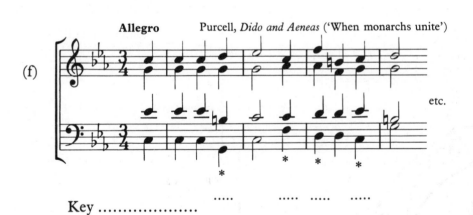

Key ....

Key ....

▎ Composing a melody

In Grade 5 you will be asked to compose a short melody, lasting not more than eight bars. There will be a choice between composing for an instrument or for voice. If you choose the former, you will have the option of selecting one from a number of specified instruments (e.g. violin, cello, clarinet, trumpet). They will all be capable of playing melodies of the type to be discussed below, and you will not need a detailed knowledge of any of them. Nevertheless, you should keep in mind the basic characteristics of the instrument you choose. If you write for the violin, for example, you may wish to include some pizzicato notes, assuming that they are appropriate to the style of the melody. It is particularly important to keep in mind the lowest note which the instrument can play. (See *The AB Guide to Music Theory* Part II, Chapters 19–20 for this information.)

A melody for an instrument will have a given opening. One for voice will have given words but not a given opening. Bear in mind that voices usually have much smaller ranges than instruments: it would be sensible to keep within a range of a 12th.

Irrespective of whether it is written for an instrument or for voice, some general advice can be given about the type of melody required:

(1) Notice that the syllabus says 'not more than eight bars' (these include the given opening in an instrumental melody). In the early stages at least, there is much to be said for aiming at exactly eight bars, since eight-bar melodies are very common and the easiest to compose. Many well-known songs, old and new, provide examples, but others are to be found in purely instrumental music.

(2) Your melody should be self-contained: it should not be left at a point where something more is required to finish it.

(3) Performance directions should be included (although a simple eight-bar melody is unlikely to need many). The following points are a guide:

(i) Start by deciding how fast you want the melody to be performed, and add a tempo direction (e.g. *Allegro*, *Andante* or a metronome mark).

(ii) Show the dynamic level (*mf*, *p* etc.) which you think suitable. If, during the course of the melody, you want to vary the speed or the dynamic level, give the necessary instructions (e.g. *rit.*, ⟨ etc.).

(iii) Add phrasing (articulation) marks, e.g. legato slurs and staccato dots. Care is needed in drawing slurs. It must always be clear which note they start from, and at which note they end: vague sweeps will not do. If (as in these melodies) there is only one voice or instrument on the stave, a slur is normally placed on the same side as the note-heads when these all go in the same direction. Where there is a mixture of upward and downward stems, the slur usually goes above the notes. Ties and staccato marks go within or below the slur – never above it.

Perhaps the most important point to stress in these preliminary remarks is the necessity of trying to hear in your mind what you have written. In the examination room, of course, you will not have access to an instrument. However, you may find it helpful to use one when practising, particularly in the early stages; and it is always a good idea to try over a melody when you have finished it, to see whether you have actually written the sounds you intended.

This test is more than a matter of working out patterns of notes on paper: it is a challenge to your inventiveness and imagination. The hints given below can do no more than provide a stimulus and a help in giving shape to your ideas.

The most important features in a melody are (i) its rhythmic organisation and (ii) the shapes produced by the pitches of its notes. Both may be illustrated by reference to some well-known melodies –

35

In planning the rhythm of the melody, you may find it useful to revise what was said about four-bar rhythms in Grade 2 (Section H) and Grade 3 (Section I) of *Music Theory in Practice*. The principles outlined there apply equally to the rhythms of eight-bar melodies (allowing for the fact that, in any references to the numbers of bars, the numbers now have to be doubled). In the melodies quoted on the previous pages, for example, you can see instances where:

(1) the rhythm of bars 1–4 is repeated exactly in bars 5–8 –

(2) the two halves are very nearly but not exactly the same –

(3) the two halves start the same but finish differently –

(4) the two halves start differently but finish the same, or very nearly so –

(5) the opening rhythm is used again in the second quarter of the tune –

(6) the melody does not divide into *equal* sections: 'Nymphs and shepherds' consists of 3 + 5 bars, with the opening rhythm occurring again in bar 4 –

(i)

When an opening rhythm occurs again later in a melody, its notes too may occur again, i.e. the repetition of the music is exact, as in Examples (d) and (i). There is always a danger, however, that an absolutely exact repetition will sound boring. To avoid this, the pattern of the notes may be modified, e.g. in Example (b) where the notes are all moved down one degree –

Notice also that each half of this tune contains another rhythmic repetition –

Here, the notes in the second half (bars 6–8) do not follow those in the first half (bars 2–4); however, the three descending quavers at the start of bar 3 are matched by three descending quavers at the start of bar 7 –

Exact or modified repetitions of the opening music occur most frequently at the start of the second half of the melody, as in Example (d). They are also common at the beginning of the second quarter, as in Example (g) –

Repetitions of whatever kind help to make a melody hold together, but they are not essential. What is always important, though, is the *overall* shape produced by the notes. In this connection, two points may usefully be made. The first is that a melody should have a sense of direction. 'While shepherds watched', for example, gradually moves upwards until it reaches the D, and then gradually comes down again. Very approximately one can say that the first half of the melody is an ascent, and the second half a descent: upward movement is balanced by downward movement. But neither half goes *straight* up or straight down. Both halves contain smaller ascents and descents. This is but one possible shape, however: there is no necessity to reach a high point half-way through a melody, and the particular ways in which ascending and descending movement may be balanced and contrasted are infinitely varied. The only thing which is always poor is an aimless circling around the same few notes.

The second point concerns cadences, and the chords which they imply. Apart from some folksongs and other special cases, most melodies are inseparably connected with their supporting harmonies, and nowhere more so than at the cadence points. Thus, the final note of a melody will belong to the tonic chord (the chord with which most compositions almost always end), and will usually be the tonic note itself. The chord most commonly found at a cadence during the course of a melody (generally half-way through) will be the dominant. Notice that, in most of the melodies (a) to (i) above, the note at the half-way point belongs to the dominant chord – though it is not necessarily the dominant note itself. (These points have been shown by a 'V' printed below the melody.)

A melody set to words needs to be shaped in the same way as a purely instrumental melody. Nevertheless, there are both advantages and disadvantages in choosing to compose a melody to words. The big advantage is that the words themselves may suggest musical ideas – mood, rhythmic patterns, pitch shape, and so on. The disadvantage is that the melody must fit the words, and it will be partly judged by its suitability as a setting of them. This is a matter which goes beyond the problems of setting words to suitable rhythms, which were discussed in Section G of *Music Theory in Practice*, Grade 4. For example, the character of the melody must be suitable to the mood of the words: a bright and cheerful melody would clearly be unsuitable for sad words. Similarly, the shape of the melody should help to highlight the important words.

As illustrations, two settings are given below of a verse by Allan Cunningham. Its rhythmic aspect was discussed in *Music Theory in Practice*, Grade 4 (Section I). 'Version 4' given there is used in both the following settings: i.e. their rhythms are identical. The first setting adds emphasis to certain words (cold, snow, sleep, prim[roses]), by placing them at the tops of curves in the melody, with 'sleep' as the highest note of all. The second setting is poor because there is no such match: the shape of the melody does nothing to bring out the meaning of the words; and its high point (the top G) is particularly inappropriate on a weak syllable.

Both of these settings are entirely 'syllabic': i.e. each syllable has only one note. However, syllables may of course be set to two or more notes –

This can help to bring out the meaning of the words – but be warned: it can also do precisely the opposite! Here, as always, it is important to try and hear what you write. There is nothing worse than pointless complications.

When you work the next two exercises, remember that only the clef and the key signature should be shown at the beginning of the second and later staves – *not* the time signature. The only exception is when there is a change of time signature at the start of a new stave – and then the time signature should also be shown after the bar-line at the end of the previous stave.

Exercise 33 Compose melodies of not more than eight bars, using the following openings and writing for one of the given instruments in each case. You may substitute a different clef for the one given, provided it is appropriate to the selected instrument. Performance directions (tempo, phrasing, dynamics etc.) should be included.

Exercise 33
(continued)

(c)

for flute, oboe
or clarinet

(d)

for viola, clarinet
or horn

(e) for violin, oboe
or clarinet

(f) for cello, bassoon
or trombone

for violin, oboe
or clarinet

for oboe, horn
or trumpet

for viola, clarinet
or bassoon

for violin, flute
or oboe

Exercise 33
(continued)

(k)  for cello, horn
or trombone

(l)  for violin, flute
or trumpet

(m)  for violin, viola
or trumpet

(n) 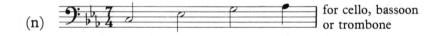 for cello, bassoon
or trombone

Exercise 34   Compose melodies of not more than eight bars to the following words. Make sure that each syllable is clearly placed under the note or notes to which it belongs. Indicate the appropriate speed and other necessary performance directions.

(a)   But slumber hold me tightly till I waken in the dawn,
And hear the thrushes singing in the lilacs round the lawn.   *Robert Louis Stevenson*

(b)   For I dipt into the future, far as human eye could see,
Saw the Vision of the world, and all the wonder that would be.   *Alfred Tennyson*

(c)   I shall remember while the light lives yet,
And in the night time I shall not forget.   *Algernon Swinburne*

Exercise 34
(continued)

(d) The day begins to droop,
  Its course is done:
But nothing tells the place
  Of the setting sun.   *Robert Bridges*

(e) Who has seen the wind?
  Neither you nor I:
But when the trees bow down their heads
  The wind is passing by.   *Christina Rossetti*

(f) The Camel's hump is an ugly lump
Which well you may see at the Zoo;
But uglier yet is the Hump we get
From having too little to do.   *Rudyard Kipling*

(g) A flea met a fly in a flue,
     Said the flea let us fly,
     Said the fly let us flee,
     So they flew through a flaw in the flue.   *Nursery Rhyme*

(h) Young Ben he was a nice young man,
        A carpenter by trade;
     And he fell in love with Sally Brown,
        That was a lady's maid.   *Thomas Hood*

(i) April, April,
     Laugh thy golden laughter;
     Then, the moment after
     Weep thy golden tears!   *William Watson*

Exercise 34
(continued)

(j)   Only a man harrowing clods
      In a slow, silent walk,
  With an old horse that stumbles and nods
      Half asleep as they stalk.   *Thomas Hardy*

(k)   Wee folk, good folk,
      Trooping all together;
  Green jacket, red cap,
      And white owl's feather!   *William Allingham*

(l)   This is
  Where the river
  Runs down to the sea,
  Listen to its music, hear this mystery! *Sacheverell Sitwell*
      © From 'Grande Sicilienne' published by Duckworth & Co.

J Ornaments

(see *The AB Guide to Music Theory*, 12/1–2)

The new requirement in Grade 5 is to replace written-out ornaments by ornament signs.

For example, 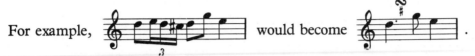 would become .

Do not be confused by the fact that there may be other possible interpretations of the appropriate ornament apart from the one given: e.g. the above turn might also be played

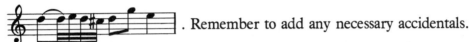 . Remember to add any necessary accidentals.

Exercise 35   Rewrite the following passages using ornament signs to replace the notes in brackets.

Reproduced by permission of Editions Hamelle, Paris/United Music Publishers Ltd

K Chords at cadential points

(see *The AB Guide to Music Theory*, 9/2)

You will be asked to choose chords for a simple melody in C, G, D or F major. Only the chords on the tonic, supertonic, subdominant and dominant (I, II, IV and V) will be needed. They will be used at points in the melody where there is a cadence.

The chords most commonly used at cadences are:

V followed by I (making a 'perfect' cadence);
IV followed by I (a 'plagal' cadence);
any chord followed by V (an 'imperfect' cadence).
In Grade 5, therefore, an imperfect cadence may be I–V, II–V or IV–V.

You may also have to choose a chord to go before the two cadence chords.

There are various ways in which you can indicate a chord in this question. You can:

(1) use roman numerals ('I', 'V' etc.) or
(2) show how it might appear in jazz and other popular music (e.g. 'Dm'), or
(3) add a figured bass, or
(4) write out the notes in full on the staves.

Any way will be acceptable, provided it is clear what you mean.

Using the chords listed above, most degrees of the major scale can be harmonised in two ways, but for two notes (the 3rd and the 7th degrees) there are no alternatives. These are the possibilities in C major:

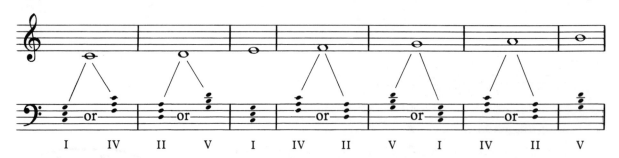

In selecting your chords, it will help you to notice these points:

(1) It is not always suitable to give every melody note one chord. A long melody note may have two chords –

Perfect Cadence V – I
Imperfect – I – V
Plagal – IV – I Amen
Interrupted – – VI

or one chord may be fitted to two or more melody notes –

Generally, chords change less often than melody notes.

(2) Sometimes there are notes in a melody which do not belong to the chords underneath. For example, two melody notes which belong to the chords may be linked by a note which does not fit the harmony. The notes marked * here are examples –

Such notes are called 'passing' notes. There must not be a gap between a passing note and the harmony note on either side of it.

(3) A similar situation occurs when a harmony note in the melody is played twice, with the next note above or below it played in between. Again, the notes marked * are examples –

Notes of this kind are called 'auxiliary' notes.

Exercise 36   Choose suitable chords for the places marked ⌐1——⌐ ⌐2——⌐ etc. in the following melodies. You may indicate the chords in any of the ways described above.

Traditional, 'Here we go round the mulberry bush'

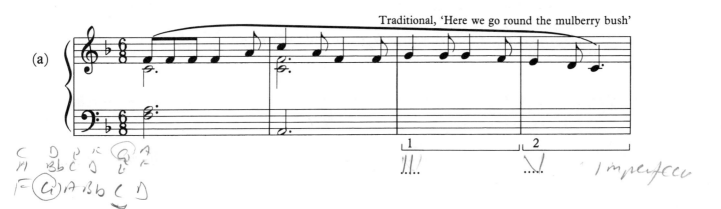

(a)

Exercise 36
(continued)

L Performance directions

In Grade 5 you will be expected to know the meaning of the following Italian terms.

attacca	go straight on to the next section of music
dolente	sad, mournful
dolore	grief (*doloroso*: sorrowful)
doppio movimento	twice as fast
estinto	as soft as possible, lifeless
incalzando	getting quicker
lacrimoso	sad
loco	at the normal pitch (used to cancel an *8va* direction)
lunga	long (*lunga pausa*: long pause)
lusingando	coaxing, in a sweet and persuasive style
misura	measure (*alla misura*: in strict time; *senza misura*: in free time)
ossia	or, alternatively
piacevole	pleasant
piangevole	plaintive, in the style of a lament
pochettino, poch.	rather little
rinforzando, rf, rfz	reinforcing
segue	go straight on
smorzando, smorz.	dying away in tone and speed
teneramente, tenerezza	tenderly, tenderness
tosto	swift, rapid (but often used in the same sense as *troppo*)
volante	flying, fast

You will also be expected to know the meaning of the following German terms.

aber	but
Ausdruck	expression
bewegt	with movement, agitated
breit	broad, expansive
ein	a, one
einfach	simple
etwas	somewhat, rather
fröhlich	cheerful, joyful
immer	always
langsam	slow
lebhaft	lively
mässig	at a moderate speed
mit	with
nicht	not
ohne	without
ruhig	peaceful
schnell	fast
sehr	very
süss	sweet
traurig	sad
und	and
voll	full
wenig	little
wieder	again
zart	tender, delicate
zu	to, too

You should also understand the signs used to show reiterations and repeats (see *The AB Guide to Music*, 13)

M Instruments and voices

In Grade 5 you will be expected to know the names of instruments, the clefs they use, instrument family groups and the basic way by which they produce sound. Section L in *Music Theory in Practice*, Grade 4, provides some basic facts; and Chapters 19–21 in *The AB Guide to Music Theory*, Part II, gives further information, although more than you will need to know at this stage.

The questions about a passage of music may include questions on voices and the clefs they use. See Section E of this book for some basic facts and Chapter 14 in *The AB Guide to Music Theory*, Part II, for more detailed information.

N General exercises

(handwritten notes in top margin)

Exercise 37 The following passage is the opening of a piece, *Berceuse*, by the Russian composer, Ilynsky. Look at it, and then answer the questions below.

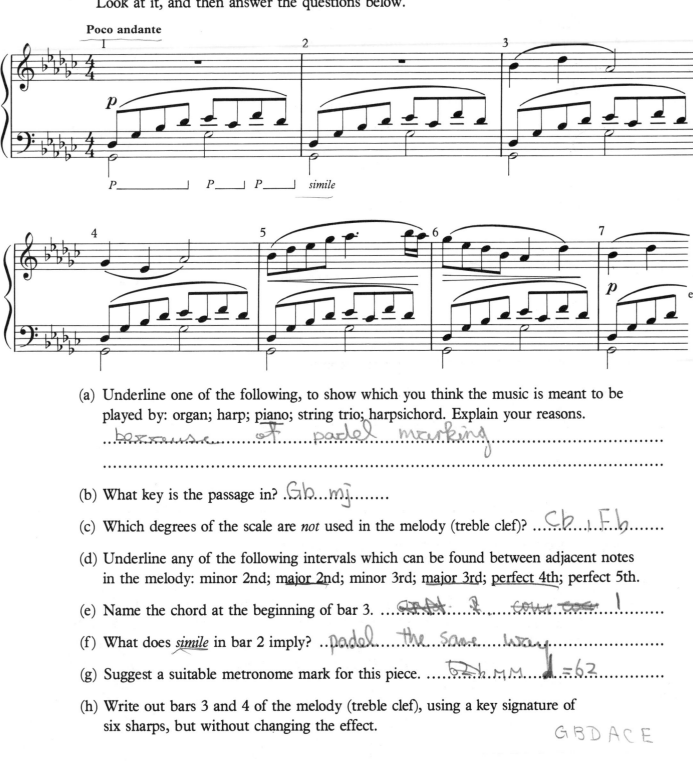

(a) Underline one of the following, to show which you think the music is meant to be played by: organ; harp; <u>piano</u>; string trio; harpsichord. Explain your reasons.
because of padel marking

(b) What key is the passage in? *Gb mj*

(c) Which degrees of the scale are *not* used in the melody (treble clef)? *Cb . Fb*

(d) Underline any of the following intervals which can be found between adjacent notes in the melody: minor 2nd; <u>major 2nd</u>; minor 3rd; <u>major 3rd</u>; <u>perfect 4th</u>; perfect 5th.

(e) Name the chord at the beginning of bar 3. *(handwritten)*

(f) What does *simile* in bar 2 imply? *padel the same way*

(g) Suggest a suitable metronome mark for this piece. *MM ♩ =62*

(h) Write out bars 3 and 4 of the melody (treble clef), using a key signature of six sharps, but without changing the effect.
GBDACE

Exercise 38 The following passage is the opening of the second movement of Beethoven's Trio for 2 oboes and cor anglais. Look at it, and then answer the questions below.

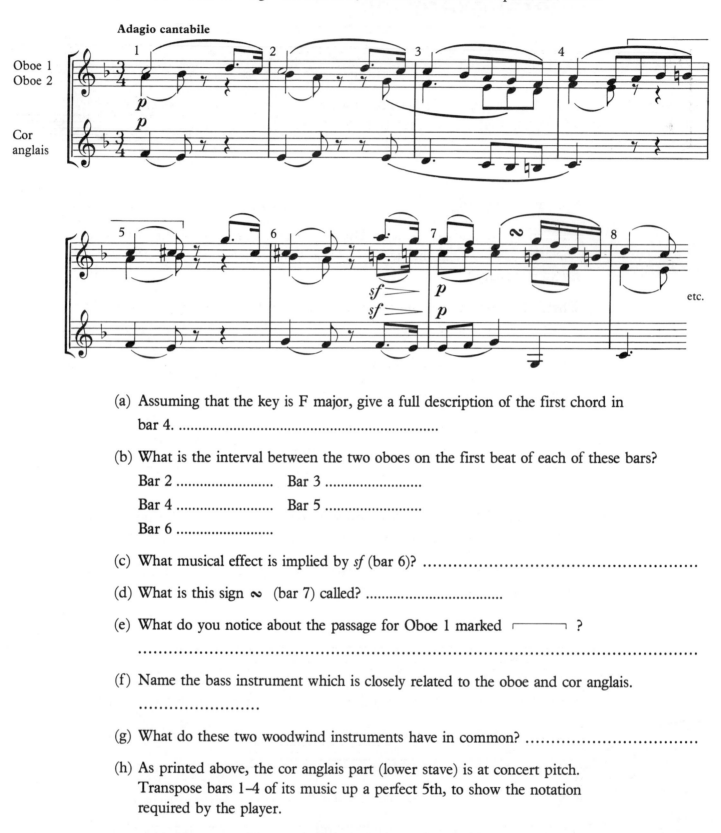

(a) Assuming that the key is F major, give a full description of the first chord in bar 4. ....

(b) What is the interval between the two oboes on the first beat of each of these bars?

Bar 2 .... Bar 3 ....

Bar 4 .... Bar 5 ....

Bar 6 ....

(c) What musical effect is implied by *sf* (bar 6)? ....

(d) What is this sign ∾ (bar 7) called? ....

(e) What do you notice about the passage for Oboe 1 marked ⌐‾‾‾⌐ ?

....

(f) Name the bass instrument which is closely related to the oboe and cor anglais.

....

(g) What do these two woodwind instruments have in common? ....

(h) As printed above, the cor anglais part (lower stave) is at concert pitch. Transpose bars 1–4 of its music up a perfect 5th, to show the notation required by the player.

Exercise 39   The following passage is for 4-part choir. It comes at the end of a motet, *Ave verum*, by Mozart (the words are not shown.) Look at it, and then answer the questions below.

(a) Explain the meaning of SATB. ....

(b) The key of the motet is D major. Draw a ring round any notes in the passage which are chromatic in this key. (Note that some of the accidentals are not strictly necessary.)

(c) What is the interval between the highest note and the lowest note in the melody (top line of the music)? ....

(d) What is the largest interval between the two upper voices? ....

(e) What is the smallest interval between the two lower voices? ....

(f) Name the chords above the bass notes marked (i), (ii) and (iii).

   (i) ....   (ii) ....   (iii) ....

(g) Which note is sung in unison by two of the voices? ....

(h) Name two orchestral instruments which could play the bass part of this passage.
   ....cello........ and .....piano.....

(i) Write out bars 5–6 in open score, using the appropriate clefs. Remember to put in the key signatures.

Exercise 40   The following passage is from the last movement of Ravel's String Quartet, printed here on two staves (i.e. in short score). Look at it, and then answer the questions below.

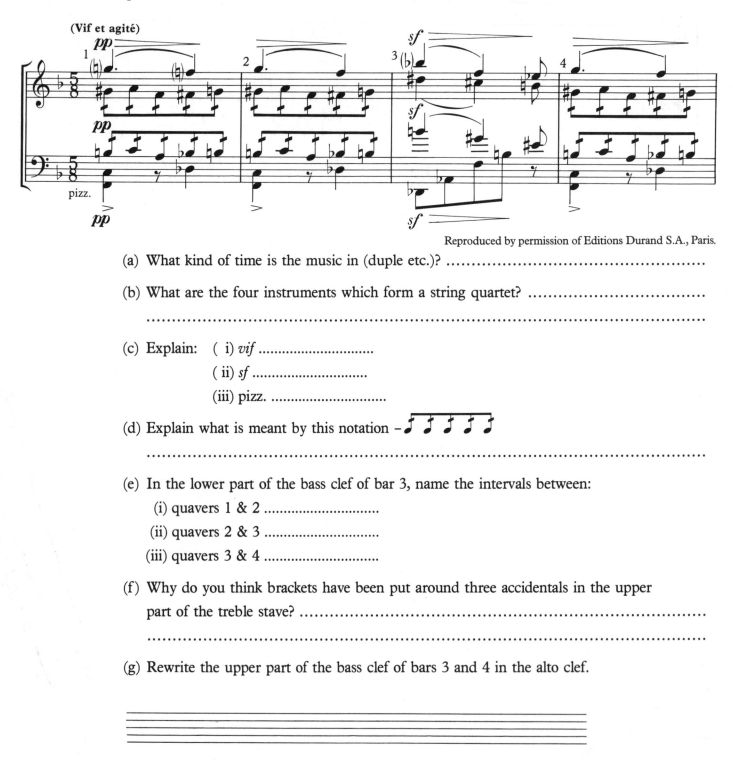

(a) What kind of time is the music in (duple etc.)? ....

(b) What are the four instruments which form a string quartet? ....

....

(c) Explain: (i) *vif* ....
              (ii) *sf* ....
              (iii) pizz. ....

(d) Explain what is meant by this notation –

(e) In the lower part of the bass clef of bar 3, name the intervals between:
    (i) quavers 1 & 2 ....
    (ii) quavers 2 & 3 ....
    (iii) quavers 3 & 4 ....

(f) Why do you think brackets have been put around three accidentals in the upper part of the treble stave? ....

....

(g) Rewrite the upper part of the bass clef of bars 3 and 4 in the alto clef.